Ball of Confusion in Galatia
Fighting a Religious, Nationalistic,
and Ethnic Battle

By Jimmie D. Compton, Jr.

Dedication

To my wife Nancy, for calmly and quietly supporting what must have appeared as a year-long writing obsession. May the Lord shower you with blessings for allowing me to hear Him in peace and with clarity.

A special thanks to Dr. Barbara Brooks, Carolyn Drew, and Cedric Wright for your devotion—from sunrise to sunset of Hope Bible Fellowship Church—to her gospel service, giving, teaching, and communication ministries.

Published by Jimmie Davis Compton, Jr.

Printed in the United States of America

Publisher's Cataloging-in-Publication Data

Compton, Jimmie Davis, Jr., 1951-

Ball of confusion in Galatia: Fighting a religious, nationalistic, and ethnic battle / Jimmie D. Compton, Jr.

ISBN: 978-0-940123-12-0

This book highlights how Jesus and the Apostle Paul provided their faith communities with clarity during the cultural mishmash of ideological confusion during their day, while maintaining the ethos, pathos, and logos of the kingdom of God. The hope is, by examining how they confronted the various violent, religiously nationalist, ethnically biased, imperialistic, and corrupt ideologies of their day, that twenty-first century church leaders can develop roadmaps for discipling their faith communities into the salt and light of the world, without them becoming as the world.

First Edition

Cover photo by Jimmie D. Compton, Jr.

Table of Contents

Introduction

This book provides twenty-first century Christians with a few kingdom principles for navigating through today's assortment of religious, ethnic, moral, political, and social beliefs that oppose or slightly deviate from what we believe to be biblical. References to Jesus' earthly ministry and Apostle Paul's letter to the church at Galatia are cited as effective use of kingdom principles for bringing clarity to our divisiveness today.

In a somewhat *in-between-the-lines* fashion, the New Testament reveals the ethos, pathos, and logos with which both Jesus and the Apostle Paul sought to establish and sustain kingdom-centered faith communities (churches) within an ideologically diverse culture. Here are brief descriptions of terms:

Ethos: The manner in which their authority or credibility is evident through their deeds, beliefs and aspirations.

Pathos: Their emotional response to a passionate plea, or convincing accounts.

Logos: The way they reasoned with others; using history, facts, parables, figures (individual and objects), and rationale.

We can only imagine the difficulty the members of those new faith communities had in mastering these intangible virtues, while in the midst of very present adversaries. Certainly, Jesus' and Paul's preaching, teaching, healing, evangelism, outreach, and knowledge of Old Testament history was solid. However, ethos, pathos, and logos arise from a deeper and endearing mode of operation within. Unfortunately, I cannot say that they enthusiastically lived out these virtues. But I can say that Jesus and Paul did embrace them.

This book is not an exposition on Paul's letter to the Galatians, nor does it provide a guaranteed formula for remedying conflicts. What is presented are observations of legacy Christian ethos, pathos, and logos that believers today should embrace, in order to maintain our integrity as the salt and light of this confused world.

Cultural confusion is not unique to today's generation. To be honest, it is unlikely that solving the confusion in America will come as a result of reading this book. References to today's confusion are made simply to demonstrate a few high-level similarities to those in first-century Galatia, but not to suggest that there are similarities in the details.

Jesus' perspective about human need differed from Jewish/Samaritan hate, Rome's geo-political views, the Pharisees' national-religious views, the Zealots' political views, and the Herodians' dynastic ambition. His beliefs about sicknesses and diseases such as leprosy, palsy, blindness, etc., also differed. Similarly, Apostle Paul was summoned to bring clarity to the confusion in Galatia that had been brought on by well-meaning Messianic-Jewish[1] infiltrators and their national-ethnic message (described in more detail in Chapter 4). Paul's letter in response to the confusion attempted to vindicate both himself as an apostle and the truth of his *Jesus plus nothing else* gospel message.

This book wraps up with take-aways—a reminder to Christians today to remain unified in the essential matters of the faith, and to give liberty in non-essential matters.[2] Finally, the hope is that, in humility we will trust our invisible God's undisclosed detailed plans for the balance of human history. And also, to trust the Holy Spirit to transform others, rather than attempt to manufacture outcomes through human efforts.

"For it is the work of divine wisdom ... to ensure that whatever happens through the evils hatched by someone, a good and useful result will come of it."

- Clement of Alexandria

Chapter 1: The Look of Cultural Confusion

People moving out, people moving in
Why? Because of the color of their skin
Run, run, run but you sure can't hide

An eye for an eye, a tooth for a tooth
Vote for me, and I'll set you free
Rap on, brother, rap on

Well, the only person talking about love thy brother is the preacher
And it seems nobody's interested in learning, but the teacher

Segregation, determination, demonstration, integration

Aggravation, humiliation, obligation to our nation

Ball of confusion
That's what the world is today

Growing Up in Confusion

That was the jam! The 1970 Motown song "Ball of Confusion" by the Temptations. It was recorded and produced in my hometown Detroit by Motown Records, when I was eighteen years old. At the risk of dating myself, I can relate to each stanza in the opening lyrics above. I actually lived through the confusion that resulted from those events. Indulge me as I stray a bit:

People moving out, people moving in. Why? Because of the color of their skin: My father was part of America's Great Migration from the Jim Crow south for the automotive job opportunities in Detroit. We were the first black family in a neighborhood mixed with Italians, Germans, a Chinese family, and a few "good ole boys" from the south, whose families thought they owned America. Our family had ringside seats to Detroit's white flight!

As young teens, my brother worked at the Famous Italian Bakery on Shoemaker Street, and I worked at the corner store on Lemay and

Shoemaker for a German butcher named Harry. He was the right man for those very generous times. Harry allowed customers (my parents included) to run up a bill throughout the week. Customers could then pay their bill at a designated time.

An eye for an eye, a tooth for a tooth. Vote for me, and I'll set you free: For the most part, the people in our neighborhood were kind and generous. However, my older sisters would not hesitate to return viciousness whenever our family had been victimized. In the 1950s, they even fought to defend me during desegregation, as we walked to elementary school. The first time I can recall collective sadness was when my father, along with many other black people, had hope that the campaign promises of John F. Kennedy would materialize when he was elected President of the United States. Those hopes were dashed by his assassination while I was in junior high school.

Well, the only person talking about love thy brother is the preacher. And it seems nobody's interested in learning, but the teacher: When it came to both church and school, neither my body nor my mind was interested in learning. Periodically, my mom played the piano for True Rock Baptist Church, and my sisters attended

East Grand Boulevard Methodist Church. My brother and I simply had fun playing wherever we happened to be, while the others family members were away.

Rather than feed us religion, our father, a talented, very intelligent and effective provider, sat all of us down and read from two huge picture books. One was entitled, *The Epic of Man*. Bait, hook, line and sinker, I took it all in! I was not confused, because I knew nothing about the Lord or the Bible. From childhood, I had been set on the path of a skeptic that eventually led to a bachelor's degree in Anthropology and Sociology.

Although my sisters received good grades in school, my brother and I did not. Since grade school, the only time I took coursework seriously was when the teachers uttered the dreaded words, "Report cards go out next week." I then began to try very hard, but to no avail—a few days just was not enough time for me to improve my grades to an acceptable mark.

Segregation, determination, demonstration, integration, aggravation, humiliation, obligation to our nation: I started Hutchinson Elementary in 1956, a year after desegregation. It was apparent to me that I was not wanted there, but I never attributed that to my race. I just felt that the principal and some teachers were mean and hateful. I am grateful to have had experienced joy and approval along with my siblings, as we huddled around the radio listening to the Canadian radio station CKLW. During those days, it was the only station that played Motown songs. Local stations did not play them.

In 1963, my father made a poster to hold up as he participated in Detroit's Walk to Freedom. At the time, it was the largest civil rights demonstration in our nation's history. This demonstration was where Rev. Dr. Martin Luther King, Jr. first gave his famous "I Have a Dream" speech. Then came the fireworks.

Four years later, in 1967, while my sister and I sat in the Fox Theater watching the Motown Revue, a riot broke out. Within days, troops were marching down our street. Forty-three people died, many more were injured, seven-thousand people were arrested, and more than one thousand buildings were burned. On a grassroots level, we witnessed what fueled not only the riot, but also boosted the Black Power movement. Then tragically, in 1968, over our high school's public address system, came the announcement about Dr. Martin Luther King, Jr's assassination. My classmates and I left school for a five-mile protest march to Wayne State University's campus. These were very troublesome days.

Some might say, "That's only how black Americans experienced the times." They might have had a point, except just five years prior to the release of "Ball of Confusion," Barry McGuire's 1965 song "Eve of Destruction" had already flooded the airways. A lyric from his song went like this:

> Yeah, my blood's so mad, feels like
> coagulatin'
> I'm sittin' here just contemplatin'
> I can't twist the truth, it knows no
> regulation
> Handful of senators don't pass legislation
> And marches alone can't bring integration
> When human respect is disintegratin'
> This whole crazy world is just too
> frustratin'
> And you tell me
> Over and over and over again, my friend
>
> How you don't believe
> We're on the eve of destruction

When Confusion Became Personal

To my disappointment, "Ball of Confusion" hit the airways just as I received notice from the United States Selective Service to report for a military draft physical. There I was, a young black adult with no faith, treated unfairly in grade school, not accepted as a boy scout, discriminated against, and now required to put my life on the line in the Vietnam War. It had already taken the lives of some of my classmates and neighbors. It had turned my childhood friend from across the alley into an addict. He was the best baseball catcher I had ever seen. Confusion about what to fight for, the rights of my people or America's interest in the Middle-East haunted me daily.

Sorry, but I have to interject this testimony. After eighteen years of living through all of this confusion, only in hindsight and having done nothing to deserve it, can I say that the Lord sent me a ram in a bush. I was awarded a football scholarship to Southern University. It made me eligible for a Selective Service student deferment. All I had to do was stay in college and maintain good grades. In 1970, there I was, in Baton Rouge, Louisiana on Southern University's campus, majoring in computer science, given the nickname Motown by dormmates, and I had a new motivation to improve my grades. Back home almost a year later, I met the woman who brought more order, structure, and purpose into my life. Shortly thereafter, I had a coincidental reunion with a previous coworker who later led me to accept Jesus Christ.

Okay, back to general confusion back then and now!

We're Still Living in Confusion

You must agree, the songs "Ball of Confusion" and "Eve of Destruction" are just as relevant now as ever! A cultural mishmash of diverse and competing viewpoints is not new. Historically, within our culture, there had existed an element of commonality among each faction that provided the unifying "glue" to keep brotherly love intact (at least enough to be civil).

As recently as 2009, our commonality still outweighed any differences in political parties, economics, ethnicity, faith, or morality. Our unifying bond could not be broken by natural disaster or by the threat of terrorist attacks like the one that occurred on September 11, 2001.[3] Unfortunately, due to disparities in how those common elements were administered within the culture, differences and diversity descended into hatred, and tolerance turned into chaos. Now, here we are.

I am suggesting that gross disparities and inequities in today's wealth, employment, justice, handling of immigrants, and government have finally dissolved the glue that once fastened the floodgates. What was once a tolerance of differences has morphed into angst. What once worked collaboratively in order to unify diversity has become chaos. Sadly, the checks and balances between our three branches of government have ceased serving the interests of "We the People ..." in order to serve the interests of a single branch–the Executive Branch. Perhaps those who are the most confused are those who once embraced the times of unity. Trying to understand how it all unraveled can be mind-boggling.

Imagine how difficult it must be for leaders of multi-generational churches. They are responsible for leading or growing their faith community through the fray that has set the American culture into chaos! Sure, pastors can manage the day-to-day affairs of the church. Yeah, they can participate in board meetings, staff meetings, meet with the Deacon board, and oversee the operation of church ministries. But what is the leader to do when congregants do not want to deny themselves and pick up their cross daily and follow Jesus? Or when a member is convinced that their political faction in the cultural chaos is the only right faction? How can a pastor convince believers to fight with kingdom weapons, not earthly ones? Pastoral aids, books, seminars, retreats, and skill assessments provide very little help.

The challenge to the church in America today is to exist within the cultural fray, in contextual ways, with the ethos, pathos, and logos that Jesus and Paul modeled. After all, Jesus called us to be salt and light. As such, we must be intentional about representing kingdom virtues within this fallen and corrupt culture. As a faith community (salt) within the culture, we are not to take the side of a particular faction in the fray. Rather, we are to show the way to the culture (light). These factions need to see how we deal with one another and with them. That is how light overcomes darkness. We are not so naïve as to believe that by doing so, others will calm down and problems will be solved. Our role is to ensure that others can see that there is another way. It is between them and the Holy Spirit that real change occurs. Do not let your "good ole' Yankee ingenuity" deceive you into trying to manufacture spiritual outcomes in others. We need to be a unified American church that keeps in step with the Spirit. Through Him, the light of Christ will expose and battle dark powers in high places.

"God also knows the secret things of the heart and foresees future events. In His long-suffering, He permits things to happen. And by means of those things that happen ... He reveals the secret evil within a person in order to cleanse him."

- Origen

Chapter 2: Confusion in America

"Is God on my side?" That is often the unspoken question that Christians in America ask about our cultural, ideological, and religious mishmash of beliefs. I suggest that it is an unanswerable question. What we should ask ourselves is, "Am I on God's side?" That question can be answered through an in-depth Bible study. Scriptures reveal that Jesus does not take sides. We want to think He does, in order to justify the side we have chosen. Then, we mistakenly believe that we are helping His cause. The truth is that, we cannot help Jesus until first we have surrendered our heart to Him. Even then, it will be *His* good deeds we will need to do, not simply the deeds that we decide to do for Him. The bottom line is, we cannot *put* Jesus on our side.

- Being a Christian nationalist who does not condone liberal Christians does not put the Lord on your side.

- Being against the union of the church and the State does not put the Lord on your side.

In fact, not being broken and contrite about the sinful indulgences and the ungodly motives of our personal, private, and secret lives, places us closer to Satan than to Jesus.

The Church and the Cultural Fray

When we as Christians get caught up in the cultural chaos or confused by it, Jesus' teachings can help us re-center our perspective around the idea of having a side. Here is what He teaches about

The side a wise person takes.

> Therefore everyone who hears these words of mine and puts them into practice is like a wise man who built his house on the rock. The rain came down, the streams rose, and the winds blew and beat against that house; yet it did not fall, because it had its foundation on the rock. (Matthew 7:24-25)

Loving our heavenly Father and loving others (even those with opposing viewpoints).

> Jesus replied: "Love the Lord your God with all your heart and with all your soul and with all your mind." This is the first and greatest commandment. And the second is like it: "Love your neighbor as yourself." All the Law and the Prophets hang on these two commandments. (Matthew 22:37-40)

What does loving others look like.

> So in everything, do to others what you would have them do to you, for this sums up the Law and the Prophets. (Matthew 7:12)

Jesus is the standard and the side to embrace! The more obedient we are to Him rather than our feelings (our side), another person (side of others), or to our allegiance to an organization ("volun-told" side), the more sound our foundation. Remaining on His foundation in this chaotic culture will prevent any weapon forged against us from succeeding (John 15:4; Isaiah 54:17).

By taking neither side but proclaiming His own side (John 18:36), Jesus lived out the kingdom virtues that He wants us to live out during conflicts with the culture. Jesus intended His followers to be a separate faith community who lived by kingdom principles and who stood out before others like a town built on a hill. His followers were not simply a reform movement within Judaism to fix its wrongs. Therefore, above all, we are to be kingdom minded. Whether facing death, anger, slander, disagreement, or loss, we are to strive to be more concerned about the perception we are projecting about God's kingdom, than we are about our own honor (Matthew 5:21-26; also read what Paul urged the church at Corinth about the same in 1 Corinthians 6:1-9).

"Although disease, accident, and ... death come upon the spiritual man, ... by the power of God they become the medicine of salvation. ... they benefit those whose are difficult to reform."

- Clement of Alexandria

Chapter 3: Confusion in Jesus' Day

What can be learned from examining how Jesus handled interactions with the many factions of His day would fill a library. The following are brief and general descriptions of the ideologies and worldviews in and around Judea during Jesus' earthly ministry. As you read, try to lift Jesus' ethos, pathos, and logos from His interactions.

Ideologies and Views in Jesus' Day

Sadducees: They did not believe in an afterlife, resurrection, or eternal life. Perceiving their poor understanding of the Torah, the Law, and Prophetic books, Jesus simply dialogued with them to provide clarity (Matthew 22:23-33).

Pharisees: They believed in the promises of Yahweh, particularly that the Jews were His chosen people. They believed that the Torah confirmed their right to rule and to proselytize the world under Jewish authority. The Pharisees tried to trap Jesus in His own words. Instead, He convicted them with their own words, or with the Torah. Although they were well educated in the Torah, the Law and the Prophetic books, Jesus often referenced their own sacred books to dialogue with them about His pre-existence (Matthew 22:15-22, 34-46).

Herodians: Their nationalistic ambitions were to expand their Herodian dynasty throughout Judea. They were a Jewish political group who were given a grip on regional power by Rome, for supporting Roman oversight of Judea. To preserve this privilege, they sought to keep the peace between the Jewish people and Rome. Herodians did not appear to have strong religious or political convictions, unless there was something to gain personally. It would be difficult to have a serious dialogue with them.

Zealots: They had many religious views in common with the Pharisees. But they were known more for their hatred of Rome and those who collected taxes for Rome, than anything else. They simply wanted the Romans out of Judea and Jewish rule of Judea. As the most social-political militant sect that existed during Jesus' earthly ministry and thereafter, their resentment and temperament towards the Roman occupation earned them the reputation as the most violent and aggressive group in the region.

Jesus was a disappointment to many of the Zealots because they wanted revolution. But Jesus brought divine power for spiritual rebirth and reconciliation with Yahweh. By selecting Simon the Zealot as one of His disciples (Matthew 10:4; Mark 3:18; Luke 6:15; Acts 1:13), Jesus demonstrated the power of this rebirth to the Zealots and for everyone else to witness. Apparently, Simon the Zealot saw Jesus for who He really was and abandoned his former life of violence, political activism, and extremism. The power to change the hearts of men was put on display as another disciple of Jesus, Matthew the former tax collector, served along with Simon the Zealot. Before meeting Jesus, Simon the Zealot would have murdered Matthew (viewing him as a part of the unwanted Roman system). In the end, they became spiritual brothers, working side by side for the same cause – spreading the good news.

Jewish Religious Order in Effect: The authority of priests and teachers of the Law would soon diminish, being mostly out of touch with Yahweh's love and grace, as well as being blind to His prophecies about the Messiah. As a result, they failed to make a positive impact on the spiritual lives of the people.

However, Jesus was yet to bring redemption, grace, and truth to the world through the cross (John 1:17-18). Therefore, the old covenant was still in effect. So Jesus respectfully urged the people to obey what the Pharisees taught from the law of Moses (Matthew 23:2-3). With the same respect, this is also why Jesus urged the leprous Samaritan outcast whom He healed to show himself to the priest (Luke 17:11-19). Jesus' ethos and pathos here are amazing! He was not so high-minded about possessing grace and truth that He would disrespect the religious status quo. He knew the Father's kingdom plans, yet, He was emotionally mature enough to be tolerant of those who did not.

Roman Provincial Governor Pilate: He sought the interest of the Roman Empire in all dealings in the province. When brought to him for questioning, Jesus did more than speak truth to power. He educated Pilate about the limitations of earthly power and God's ultimate control over the events (John 18:33-37; 19:9-11).

Eye for an Eye Impulsivity: Peter was a fisherman who seemed to have a Zealot's temperament. When Jesus was arrested, Peter cut off the arresting soldier's ear. As if to clarify any misunderstanding about the way of the kingdom, Jesus healed the soldier, then ordered Peter to stop. Aggression was not a kingdom principle for saving people from their sins (Luke 22:47-53; John 18:10-11). Jesus understood that the devil's provocation can trick His followers into using the world's weapons.

Roman Empire: When asked whether to obey God or Caesar, the answer was easy for Jesus. Continuity in the advancement of God's kingdom agenda was of more importance than putting Caesar in his place. It would be unwise to jeopardize making an impact for the kingdom because we were jailed for not paying taxes. Instead, it is best to just give Caesar his money, so we can continue working for God's kingdom (Matthew 22:15-22). Jesus understood that money was simply a means to an end. Why should He get distracted by objections to paying the means when His father could control getting the end (as well as the means, for that matter)?

Monetary Greed: Jesus overturned the tables of the money changers and merchants in the Temple (Matthew 21:12; Mark 11:15; John 2:15). It was commonplace for the Temple courts to accommodate large crowds, especially during the celebration of the major feasts on the Jewish calendar. Money changers would set up stalls in the Temple's outer court of the Gentiles, so worshipers could exchange their currency to pay the Temple tax with the approved currency (Exodus 30:13). Merchants often sold the animals required for sacrifice right there, on site for convenience. Over time, profiting at the expense of sincere worshippers had become commonplace. Merchants began charging significantly above market value for the animals. And what was supposed to provide a one-stop-shop convenience to Jews who traveled from long distances, became a money-grab operation. This infuriated Jesus!

Being passionate about His Father's house, Jesus was righteously disgusted by the motives of the money changers and merchants, so He cleaned house. Jesus was not dealing with opposers. They had a legitimate role in Temple worship. But they needed to be chastised not just for greed, but for disrespecting the due reverence of Temple worship and feasts.

Allow me to illustrate this using an example from the 21st century. Imagine one morning driving down the street on Easter, Valentine's Day, or Mother's Day (but not Father's Day for some reason). You have seen those box trucks that people rent to sell flowers, stuffed animals, and other knick-knacks. Usually, they are conveniently parked on a vacant lot or in a parking lot. Then over the years, times become economically difficult, and money is scarce. On one Sunday, as you pull into your church's parking lot, all the prime parking spaces have been taken by those box trucks. Lined up from the box trucks all the way to the entrance of your church are tables stacked with those flowers, stuffed animals and knick-knacks. With this illustration in mind, how do you feel now? Before you answer, note that I did not ask, "What is the noble high ground you should take?" I asked, "How do you feel?"

Jesus' Eternal Perspective

Much of the confusion, disappointment, and dissonance that we Christians often experience when the Lord does not act according to our timing would not exist, had we considered eternal life as we live in time. Eternal life is not something that we receive after we are physically dead. We receive eternal life the second the Holy Spirit indwells us. Since eternal life includes the ability to perceive the kingdom of God, we can employ many of its virtues and experience its benefits in this lifetime as well.

Jesus devoted Himself to the will of the Father. He did not take the side of a particular faction. Being *in* the world but not *of* the world, He was not naïve, oblivious, nor insensitive about politics or human needs. He did not lack concern about Roman oppression, or the fact that the religious overreach of the Pharisees had burdened and depressed the people, or that the power-hungry Herodians neither cared about the people nor God, or that the widowed, sick, and disabled were left to waste away along with their skills.

Jesus knew history. He understood that hunger, poverty, corruption, immorality, greed, etc., would persist regardless of the faction in charge, or the type of government system they established. Even the best nations, and those with the most longevity, were still filled with those evils. So what would Jesus have helped to build by devoting Himself to any of those factions?

For Jesus—with eternity in view—devoting Himself to warning people to repent and embrace the kingdom of God was far more beneficial, because heaven and hell are real. To be in either for eternity is far longer than our 70 or 80 years of earthly existence. Jesus' concern was the quality of our life in eternity. What good would it be, had He solved the earthly problems described above, only for the citizens' souls to suffer in hell?

The most serious problem is that humanity is powerless against sin. The Bible has already made this clear for us today, as Matthew 1:21 tells us "She will give birth to a son, and you are to give him the name Jesus, because he will save his people from their sins."

What About the Marginalized and Vulnerable?

Do not get me wrong. Devoted community leaders, activists, and politicians are needed to secure essential resources and opportunities for the burdened, depressed, widowed, sick, disabled, hungry, and poor. The broader truth is that those devoted community leaders, activists, and politicians also need Christians who are devoted to Jesus' message of repentance. They also need to hear and receive the gospel of Christ for the forgiveness of sin. They need prayer for health, safety, and effectiveness while they are fighting on behalf of the marginalized and vulnerable. They, too, must mature spiritually and be discipled.

Just as our Lord Jesus did, we too must keep eternity in view while helping people in the present. With kingdom ethics, we help through the use of and trust in the tools, talents, and weapons that God has given us.

"Men remain in ignorance as long as they hate, and they hate unjustly as long as they remain in ignorance."

- Tertullian

Chapter 4: Sound Teaching Leaves Galatia

<u>The Gospel or a Nationalistic Message?</u>

There are biblical scholars far more insightful than I. So, I will ease out on the proverbial thin branch by saying that I have found no other situation in the Bible that comes closer to what the church in America is experiencing today, than that which the Apostle Paul addressed in his letter to the church at Galatia. By the time of his visit there, the culture was a multicultural interplay of Celtic and Greek beliefs, and religion mixed with Roman infrastructural elements. While proclaiming the gospel of Jesus Christ, Paul and Barnabas developed a thriving faith community there.

After moving on from Galatia, some believers there abandoned the gospel of Christ that they had taught for the message of Messianic-Jewish false teachers. Apparently, Paul's leaving left a void in sound teaching. The message of the false teachers, which required Galatian believers to also obey the Law of Moses, had filled the void. Their message was fundamentally different from the "Jesus plus nothing else" gospel that Paul had taught.

A cursory reading of Paul's letter in response to the confusion in the church at Galatia might lead us to think it was simply a matter of false teachers requiring the Galatian church to include obeying the Law of Moses as a condition for being saved. But compulsory obedience to the particular Mosaic laws that they stressed would have resulted in other significant disparities as well. The cultural impact, had those laws been adopted, would have created real ethnic, religious, and social turmoil within the culture of Galatia.

Paul Receives Bad News About Galatia

How were Paul and Barnabas made aware of these desertions in the first place? They had returned from their first missionary journey to give a report to their Gentile church in Antioch

(Acts 13:1-3; 14:21). While in Antioch, some Messianic-Jewish people were teaching believers there that they had to obey the law of Moses in order to be saved. This word came prior to Paul and Barnabas' trip to Jerusalem for the first Apostolic Council described in Acts 15. Here is the account of what was reported to Paul and Barnabas:

> Certain people came down from Judea to Antioch and were teaching the believers: "Unless you are circumcised, according to the custom taught by Moses, you cannot be saved." This brought Paul and Barnabas into sharp dispute and debate with them. So Paul and Barnabas were appointed, along with some other believers, to go up to Jerusalem to see the apostles and elders about this question. (Acts 15:1-2)

Unfortunately, this false teaching had already infected the church that they had established in Galatia. Perhaps with Paul and Barnabas not being there, some believers were left to ponder, *Should we believe Paul's message of the gospel? Because what these Jewish teachers are saying seems to make sense. Or should we believe the message of the Jewish teachers? They both made some very compelling points.* Despite the fact that the believers in the church at Galatia had received the Spirit, had seen miracles, and sought to live godly while Paul was among them, some had switched sides and believed the message of the Messianic-Jewish false teachers. Like a kid in a chocolate factory, it probably was very difficult for them to pick a side.

Reasons to switch from Paul's message to that of the Messianic-Jewish false teachers' may have just boiled down to being practical (and uninformed). A believer may have simply given in, thinking, *Forget it! I can't decide. But since these new teachers are here and Paul is not, I'll just take the side of the new teachers. Besides, I'm not disbelieving Paul's message. I'm just adding God's law to it. Won't Jesus be pleased with that?* This is the confusion that Paul addressed in his letter to the Galatians. He attempted to untangle the thinking of believers who pondered in confusion about where to stand.

In the next section, we will consider some of the conflicts that have caused the church in America to ponder in confusion about where to stand. Note that these are our conflicts, and not those of the first century Galatian church.

Confusion Within America's Churches

Like the supposed reasoning of the Galatian believers who switched over to the side of the new Messianic-Jewish teachers, not every

American is insightful about the ideology of the particular side they have taken. Churches are plentiful (although declining) in America, but the quality of our theology has declined even faster. I equate the effects of our decline in teaching theology to that of those Galatians who abandoned the gospel teaching after Paul and Barnabas left. Congregants are left unequipped to know how to separate truth from invading ideologies. We are simply overwhelmed by the preponderance of ideological considerations, as well as the consequences of having chosen a particular side.

Our thinking might be, *Hey, I'm not trying to be a martyr. Besides, I have to live and work with these people.* Other believers today might take a cafeteria-style approach, like Paul's description of Apostle Peter's behavior in Galatians 2:11-14. They will pick the best from each faction, but then parrot the rhetoric of the faction that happens to be around at the time. I have seen people do this while amongst others with conflicting views about

- Compulsory Christian nationalism or universal-personal choice to surrender oneself under Jesus as Lord

- Racial supremacy or God created all humanity with equal potential

- Sexuality and gender identities or biblical male and female sexuality
- Abortion or humanity being created in the image of God
- Homosexuality as a sin or homosexuality as a life style
- No-fault divorce or biblical divorce
- Vaccination or anti-vaccination
- Capitalism or equity in the distribution of wealth
- Treating immigrants with dignity or aggressive deportation without due process
- Rolling back citizens' rights or the acceptance of diversity, equity, and inclusion
- Ethnic xenophobia or the Golden Rule
- Loyalty to my race or loyalty to my faith
- Abuse of governmental power or upholding the rule of law
- Elimination of ethics in government or holding government officials accountable

Then there are people who are unaware of their own contradictions. Though very passionate about their faction, they have not thought its beliefs through to their logical or biblical conclusions. These brew up uncertainty around what is right and wrong in the eyes of onlookers. Any student of the Bible knows that Satan does his best work where there is uncertainty. First Corinthians 14:33 reminds us that "... God is not a God of disorder but of peace—as in all the congregations of the Lord's people."

Okay, back to Paul's letter in response Galatia's confusion.

"In all trouble you should seek God. You should not set Him over against your troubles, but within them. God can only relieve your troubles if you in your anxiety cling to Him."

- Augustine of Hippo

Chapter 5: Confusion in Galatia

In Paul's response to the church at Galatia, he brings clarity to their confusion by first relying on the Lord's revelation about his calling. He makes it crystal clear that he had not preached a message of his own choosing, nor had it been influenced by the other apostles, and it certainly had not been influenced by any other human. In fact, the gospel he had preached was not even something he wanted to do! It was divinely given to him. It represented the Lord's side! Paul says in Galatians 1:13-17

> For you have heard of my previous way of life in Judaism, how intensely I persecuted the church of God and tried to destroy it. I

was advancing in Judaism beyond many of my own age among my people and was extremely zealous for the traditions of my fathers. But when God, who set me apart from my mother's womb and called me by his grace, was pleased to reveal his Son in me so that I might preach him among the Gentiles, my immediate response was not to consult any human being. I did not go up to Jerusalem to see those who were apostles before I was, but I went into Arabia. Later I returned to Damascus.

Paul portrayed himself as one time having been just as weak and ignorant of the truth as the Galatians were before they believed the gospel. His humility facilitated a common ground experience, and being transparent about his weaknesses (sins) helped make the case that his gospel was totally and exclusively dependent on the Lord. Paul took no pride in an earthly side, but revealed the Lord's call to use him to proclaim the divine side. In other words, he diminished himself, and elevated the Lord.

The Salt and Light of Paul's Response

It is important to note that in his letter to the Galatian believers, Paul did not use earthly reason, rhetoric, sayings, proverbs, or aggressive authority to bring clarity. Instead, he offered names of specific individuals, timelines, and events that could not only verify his claims, but also verify that what he offered was consistent with apostolic accountability and kingdom principles.

The purpose of his letter was twofold. First, it vindicated him as an apostle. Paul began by describing a timeline of events that attested to his apostleship and independence (not an independent message, but independent in the sense of *to whom* the message was presented: the Gentiles). To that end, he addressed the following:

- The legitimacy of his conversion, by testifying about his sins for the "traditions of my fathers" and as a persecutor of the church (1:13-14). Perhaps he hoped his testimony would serve as an example of the divine power of faith in Jesus plus nothing else. He had trusted the very Christ of the gospel that he taught the Galatians to trust.

- The authenticity of his calling (1:15-16, ref. Acts 9:1-19).

- His independence from human influence on his calling (1:16-17).

- His independence from the Judean church community's influence on his calling (1:18-24).

- His independence from influence by the pillars of the church on his calling (2:1-10).

- The admonishment he gave Peter (the "lead" apostle) for hypocrisy regarding the gospel. By implication, this also suggests his independence from Peter's influence on his calling (2:11-21).

This also served as testimony to the Galatians about how long and broadly, outside of Galatia, that the divine power of "Jesus plus nothing else" gospel had been effective at transforming souls.

Second, Paul's letter vindicated the truth of his Jesus plus nothing else gospel. He also presents evidence of the genuine power of the gospel of Jesus Christ.

- The personnel on his missionary team, Barnabas and Titus, who labored together in the Lord while proclaiming the Jesus plus nothing else gospel, was a testimony of the power of that gospel. Barnabas was a Levite (Jewish) and Titus was Greek. Together, they were unlikely companions because the training of most, if not all, Jewish leaders, priests, and Levities in the region, included learning Jewish history. This would have included the rebellion led by the Maccabees against the sacrilegious Greek Seleucid Empire, about 200 years prior. That relationship was toxic! Yet, the divine power of Paul's gospel had transformed these two to pal up and enjoy their freedom in Christ, while confronting false teachers together (2:1-5).

- Paul then brought it closer to home in Galatia. He asked a few insightful questions about how they came to believe his gospel in the first place. Of course, it was by the preached word that they received the Holy Spirit, saw miracles, and used divine power to pursue godly living. All of that was done without trying to obey the Law of Moses (3:1-6).

- Paul then used the Torah to clarify the confusion around the Messianic-Jews false teaching that required obedience to the Law of Moses. He explained that from the beginning with Abraham, it had been righteousness by faith alone (Genesis 15:6). And the law was introduced because of the existence of transgressors. Its purpose was similar to that of a babysitter who schooled us until Christ came to justify us by faith (3:23-25).

This was the twofold purpose of Paul's letter to the Galatian church.

Who Were These False Teachers?

Before diving deeper into the confusion created by these Messianic-Jews, and into Paul's response to the Galatians, there are two terms defined below that will be used throughout this book:

- First, the term *Judaizer* was coined to describe the new Messianic-Jewish false teachers who had infiltrated the church at Galatia. They taught that the Gentiles who had been converted by Paul's gospel were required to keep the Law of Moses.

- The second term is *legalism*. Not all legalism is equal. Throughout modern church history, this term has varied in meaning. But this book is only concerned with the legalism of the Judaizers in Galatia, which was quite different from the modern church's definitions for legalism today.

Today's meaning of the term legalism can vary, depending on the Christian faith community. It can mean

a. The formalization and mandating of certain Christian practices or behaviors such as church attendance, prohibition of certain vices, separation from certain types of people, political party affiliation, etc.

b. The formalization and mandating of any Christian practice or behavior. Proponents of this belief claim that the New Testament clearly identifies what is prohibited for believers, and urges us to be led by the Spirit.

c. That some Christian practices or behaviors are so edifying for believers and/or the faith community, they should be formalized and mandated, while other practices or behaviors should be left to the individual believer.

None of these modern definitions fit what was causing confusion in the church at Galatia. Nor are they the type of legalism which Paul responds to in his letter to them. Scot McKnight comes the closest to defining the kind of legalism that the Galatian church faced, which the Apostle Paul addressed. He describes it as

... a system that combined Christianity and Mosaicism in a way that demanded total commitment to Israel's law as the climax of one's conversion to Christ. This "deeper commitment to the law" according to Paul was a subversion of the adequacy of Christ's work and an abandonment of the Holy Spirit as God's way of guiding Christian ethics.[4]

The Judaizers were Messianic Jews (followers of The Way), but they added the requirement to obey the Law of Moses. Ironically, when truth is incomplete, it can contribute to confusion. In the case of the Judaizers, although they taught truth from the Torah, the Law and the prophets, and they believed in Jesus, they had not contextualized the significance of Jesus' death, burial, and resurrection as these related to those other sources of truth. Therefore, the Judaizers' understanding of God's revelation was incomplete. Their claim that God gave the Law to the Jews was true and verifiable using the Old Testament. Unfortunately, the Old Testament ends while God's revelation was still unfolding. Apparently, Jesus' redemptive work on the cross and the role of the Holy Spirit in the life of believers, went over the heads of the Judaizers. This is why Paul described the Judaizers' message as a new and different gospel (1:6-7).

"The wicked exist in this world either to be converted or that through them the good may exercise patience."

- Augustine of Hippo

Chapter 6: Saturation of the Judaizers' Legalism

On the surface, it appears that the threat of the Judaizers was only due to their insistence on obeying the Law of Moses. However, in his commentary, Scot McKnight identifies an "undertow" of threats beneath the mandate of obedience to the Law of Moses. This legalistic undertow would spread deep and wide throughout the Galatian culture. McKnight describes the potential saturation of the Judaizers' message not only as a nullifier of Jesus' redemptive work, but also as being nationalistic-racial, culturally imperialistic, and highly pragmatic.[5]

The following describes the undertow of confusion that would have resulted from the spread of the Judaizers' message:

- *Nullifies Jesus' redemptive work,* in that, including the obedience to the Law would nullify the cross of Christ as the means of God's justification of believers. Also, there would be no salvation by grace, through their faith. It would also negate the need for believers to be led by the Holy Spirit as the means for guiding them to meeting the intent of the Law.

   The basis of Paul's admonishment of those deserting the gospel (3:2, 5; 5:4) for the message of the Judaizers is based on what we know today as the Bible's teachings on justification by faith alone, the unmerited favor of God, and the sufficiency and universality of Christ's work.[6]

- *Nationalistic-ethnic,* in the sense that this was at the core of the matter between Paul and the Judaizers. The Judaizers viewed the Law as God's gift to the Jewish people, and therefore, one must embrace the Law in order to be accepted by God.[7] What is interesting is that the particular Mosaic laws to which the Judaizers required obedience were primarily those laws that differentiated the Jewish world from the Gentile world: circumcision (2:3; 5:6; 6:12), diet (2:11-14), and observing the Jewish calendar for feasts (4:10). Here is where it seems like I am splitting hairs about the nationalistic interest of these Judaizers. For them, it was not a matter of requiring obedience to the Law of Moses instead of worshipping the pagan gods of Galatia (suggesting a nationalistic-religion interest), because both the Judaizers and the church in Galatia had accepted the gospel of Christ. When we look at the particular Mosaic laws that Paul had rebuffed in his letter, it suggests that the Judaizers had focused on those Mosaic laws that differentiated the Jews from Gentiles (suggesting a nationalistic-ethnic interest).

Through these specific laws, a Jewish person's devout commitment to the Law of Moses could be seen by others (an attribute of a Pharisee, Matthew 6:5). This stirred a false sense of satisfaction about being close and committed to God, and that others were inferior. It is similar to what some people who tithe to their church feel today. Although such an ethnic bias may have been unintended, it was no less harmful to the gospel message, and therefore it needed to be refuted.

Without a doubt, these were times that the waning Jewish identity was a great concern. This was likely in the hearts of the Judaizers. After all, John the Baptist and Jesus' message of "Repent, for the kingdom of God is at hand," was radical to the Jewish status quo struggling to maintain its identity. The Jewish faith, with its deep roots in Old Testament history and traditions with Yahweh, may have been a source of collective pride. After all, they had been walking with Yahweh for well over a millennium. Even Jesus, the Messiah, was one of them. Having been at this— "faith in the true God" thing— much longer than these converted Galatian pagans, it must have been extremely difficult for the Judaizers to accept equal standing with them. This pride likely compelled the Judaizers to keep in step with the Law of Moses rather than with the Holy Spirit. Requiring obedience to the laws that differentiated them from the Gentiles only maintained their sense of religious superiority. Ignoring those laws would mean a level ground. "God forbid!" they may have thought. But the New Covenant truth is that, a level ground for all believers is inseparable from being a new creation in Christ (2 Corinthians 5:13-19).

A similar sense of religious superiority infects America today. Fortunately, since Bibles are so widely distributed, there is a record of Jesus directly dispelling such a misconception (Matthew 20).

The Judaizers had failed to incorporate what Christ and the Spirit had done to the Mosaic Law and its national character.[8] That would have helped them grasp God's complete revelation.

The basis of Paul's admonishment to those deserting the gospel for the message of the Judaizers was not simple rhetoric or his trying to out-talk them. Rather, it was rooted in divine revelation given to Apostle Peter on diet (Acts 10:9-16), and given to Paul himself on circumcision (Romans 2:29), and about the Jewish calendar (Galatians 4:9-11).

- *Cultural Imperialism,* in the sense that requiring circumcision, obeying dietary laws, and observing the Jewish calendar would impose a Jewish culture upon the

Gentile Galatian believers' culture. In effect, in addition to the religious aspect, each Gentile convert to Christ would be forced to make a commitment to the Jewish heritage. McKnight views this as a form of cultural imperialism enmeshed in a religious system, whereby the Jewish culture is held to be superior to another.[9]

Although the health benefits from both circumcision and proper dietary choices have been well documented, these were not what Judaizers had in mind. Piety, as a believer's "religious fitness" in the sight of God, was their concern. The basis of Paul's admonishment is not only that the Judaizers were teaching a different message, but that their message was crafted in a way that served a social and racial interest.[10]

- *Highly pragmatic,* in the sense that the Judaizers' message of "grace through Christ plus the Law of Moses" was not from God. It was not based on the revelation of God, nor did it depend on the Holy Spirit. Nullifying Jesus' redemptive work on the cross and having no dependence on the Holy Spirit would leave the person only with the power of the human flesh. So for Paul, the Judaizers' message was merely manmade (see 3:3 and 6:8, 12). From the beginning of his letter, in veiled words, Paul attacked this pragmatism: "Paul, an apostle—sent not from men nor by a man, but by Jesus Christ and God the Father, who raised him from the dead— and all the brothers and sisters with me," (1:1).

Judaizers had also failed to grasp why Jesus had sent the Spirit to all believers (Jew and Gentile). Obviously, they did not understand (or accept) that the same guidance for keeping the Law as well as freedom from living in the flesh was now being obtained by following the Spirit. The believer had the Spirit to guide them in ways that cultivated obedience, fulfilled the intent of the Law, and to transform their soul.

The Role of Works and Deeds

The basis of Paul's admonishment to those deserting the gospel for the message of the Judaizers was also that believers cannot please God through their effort, sincerity, or works. Works are vital for kingdom living, but they are limited in what they can do for us. A person cannot be saved by their own good works, and once saved, they cannot please God without doing His good works (Ephesians 2:8-10). Adding the need to obey the Mosaic Law to the gospel actually subtracts the sufficiency of Christ and the Spirit from God's redemption plan. McKnight considers such a mandate to be "addition by subtraction."[11]

"That your enemies have been created is God's doing; that they hate you and wish to ruin you is their own doing. What should you say about them in your mind? 'Lord be merciful to them, ...' You are loving in them not what they are, but what you would have them to become."

- Augustine of Hippo

Chapter 7: Clarity to the Confusion in Galatia

<u>Weapons for Resolving Confusion in Galatia</u>

The Judaizer threat was that it could result in a murky, mishmash human-based system of religious, nationalistic-ethnic, and cultural interests. So the challenge to Paul was to bring clarity to the confusion in the church in Galatia before the situation worsened. The Galatians needed to clearly understand the differences between the Way (where salvation can be found) and its parent religious law community (where there is only condemnation).[12] Paul sought to restore Holy Spirit-led living in Galatia, through applying similar ethos, pathos, and logos in his letter, as Jesus had in person.

The comparison below shows why Paul said the Judaizers taught a different gospel (1:6).

Paul's Jewish/Gentile Universalistic Gospel	Judaizers' Jewish Nationalistic–Ethnic Message
Centered on Christ	Centered on Moses
Guided by the Spirit	Guided by the Law
Walk according to the Spirit	Walk according to the Flesh
Justified by faith	Justified by works of the law
Promised new covenant	Based on the Law
Blessing to repentant sinners	Curse to lawbreakers
Freedom in Christ	Slaves to the law
Mature as joint heirs with Christ	Remain as infant slaves
Become a new creation	Remain as circumcision and non-circumcision
Accepted by grace through faith	Accepted by obeying the Law
Authority and power given to the Church	Authority and power given to the Jewish nation

The Lord's Weapons Are Underestimated

The Judaizers were trying to maintain the dominance of the Jewish system, just as Christian factions today try to re-establish

America's times of greatness. But the mishmash of conflicts that the Galatians faced were different from our mishmash of conflicts. Therefore, it is unlikely that Paul's letter to the Galatian church will contain specific answers that provide clarification for today's national, cultural, ideological, and religious confusion. But that does not render his letter useless.

The basis of Paul's clarification, as well as the manner in which he responded, has application for today's church. The resources he used to strengthen the church at Galatia and to refute the Judaizers are as powerful for our use today as they were for Paul. When we consider how Paul vindicated himself and the truth of the gospel, we will discover insights about how to bring clarity to the Christian factions today.

Paul relied on the Torah, his own experiences with the Lord, inspired revelations from the Lord, divine visions from the Lord, and the Jesus plus nothing else nature of the gospel. Therein is the great value of his letter. Paul was able to bring clarity to what potentially could have become a swamp of ideologically, religious, nationalist-ethnic, and cultural imperialistic confusion. He begins his letter with testimonies about weakness in his own life and Jesus redeeming him. Then, throughout his letter, are hints of his reliance on kingdom principles, such as remaining Christ-centered, being *in* this world but not *of* this world, keeping in step with the Holy Spirit, loving people who are different, etc.

Paul Uses Pre-Canonical Christian Theology

Paul addressed the Judaizer's theological deviations from divine truth that were primarily responsible for the confusion. These were at the core of the differences between his gospel message and their message. He did not argue about the undertow of potential problems of nationalism, ethnic bias, cultural imperialism, and pragmatism that could spin-off from the primary problem. It is not that those were unimportant, but bringing clarity to the primary causes of the confusion would preclude the undertow of potential problems from manifesting. Addressing the potential undertow would be like swinging at the air, because the primary problem is what caused believers to abandon the gospel. The potential problems in the undertow were yet to present themselves, and therefore were secondary.

We do not know whether or not the Judaizers had hidden motives for presenting a different message. But let me say this: Whenever a Christian faction is disingenuous about the motives behind the position that they advocate, they will not present a theological defense for their position, as Paul did. In fact, they will distract from any theological discussion and focus on secondary or hypothetical matters, or resort to diversion tactics. They are like wolves in sheep clothing. Let's consider how Paul addressed the theological deviations at their core.

Although the New Testament manuscripts and apostolic letters were yet to be canonized, Paul used many of the events described in them to bring clarity to the confusion in Galatia. I found it similar to how we apply the principles for interpreting Scripture today. He used

- Old Testament Scripture to explain/defend his gospel message (Galatians 3:6, 10-14, 18; 4:21-23).

- The divine vision given to Peter (Acts 10:9-16) and the divine revelation inspired in himself (Romans 2:29; Galatians 4:9-11), in conjunction with the redemption context of the Old Testament's revelation to explain his gospel.

- The relatively recent events of Jesus' death, burial, and resurrection and the coming of the Holy Spirit, to explain God's intent for grace through faith—not the law of Moses—to justify a person (Galatians 2:15-21).

- The Galatians' own experiences (receiving the Spirit, seeing miracles, and seeking to live godly, all without obeying the Law of Moses) as clear evidence of the truth of his Jesus plus nothing else gospel and to refute the message of the Judaizers (Galatians 3:1-6).

Effects of Paul's Letter

Did the deserting believers in Galatia return to the Jesus plus nothing else gospel? Did the Judaizers realize their error, repent, and then embrace the Jesus plus nothing else gospel? Or did the Judaizers flee Galatia, and then teach their form of legalism elsewhere? Did Paul write a follow-up letter that was lost to oblivion, to check on the Galatian church?

We do not know the answers to those questions. We do not know what effect Paul's letter had on the Galatian believers. But that is common in ministry. Although follow-up is a best practice in ministry, it has limitations. We have not been called to engineer outcomes to completion in others. One person plants seeds of truth, another person waters them with encouragement and accountability, but God gives the increase (1 Corinthians 3:6).

However, Paul does leave the Galatian believers with a prescription for not drifting from the true gospel. Paul has the same confidence in the Holy Spirit's power to guide and comfort that Jesus had, when He could no longer be physically present with His disciples. Paul tells the church at Galatia

> So I say, walk by the Spirit, and you will not gratify the desires of the flesh. For the flesh desires what is contrary to the Spirit, and the Spirit what is contrary to the flesh. They are in conflict with each other, so that you are not to do whatever you want. But if you are led by the Spirit, you are not under the law. (5:16-18)

As free and unrestrained as that seems to us controlling westerners, that is exactly how the Lord wants it. Then, the quality of motives, devotion, and love for the Lord would be that of a person's own choosing. Our true appetite for kingdom principles (godly living) would be evident through choosing to live by them by our own volition, uncloaked by compulsory memorization, rote obedience, traditional routines, posted rules, and artificial smiles.

But here is the friction: We want to see people trained to follow a moral code, in order to be good, holy, just, and groomed, for their sake and others. Yet, Jesus is looking for souls under the conviction of the Spirit and of their own accord, who will choose Him and His ways. The former makes drones. The latter makes disciples.

This expectation that believers, of their own accord, would choose to live by the Spirit without Paul's presence, was not unique to the Galatian church. Paul had commended the believers in Phillipi for doing that very thing. He says, "my dear friends, as you have always obeyed—not only in my presence, but now much more in my absence—continue to work out your salvation with fear and trembling" (Philippians 2:12).

"What is reprehensible is that while leading good lives themselves and abhorring those of wicked men, some, fearing to offend, shut their eyes to evil deeds instead of condemning them and pointing out their malice."

- Augustine Hippo

Chapter 8: The Lord Left Us His General Plan

Our closed biblical canon does reveal several details about how Jesus Christ will return as Judge to wrap up the balance of human history. However, many of those details are cryptic. Besides, it does not provide the insight needed for *us* to sort sinners who are redeemable from sinners who are not. For that, we would have to be omniscient. This is why the church must not try to help the Lord by engineering His outcomes individually or nationally.

Jesus did not establish the church to make nations great, nor for us to live as we please, and forbid that I say, not even to fight for

69

justice, equity, and inclusion. There is a slippery-sloped tendency of the church to morph into an organization that the culture wants, or the culture believes it needs. The problem with that is, more importantly, the church is a living organism with a body and head (Romans 8:10; Galatians 2:20; Ephesians 4:1-16; Colossians 1:18).

When it comes to *knowing* what we have been called to be and what we are called to do, we are more like football tailgaters in the fall. Tailgaters come in a variety of types who bring a variety of things to the event. They have the energy. They have the hope. They have the jersey. They have the team colors. They have the grills and coolers. They have the drinks. They have an endless spread of food. Do you want to know what they do not have? The game plan.

The church does not have God's detailed plans for the balance of humanity. Therefore, its members must be careful when making character judgments about others. Such judgments are orders of magnitude beyond our intellect and insight. Instead, let's strive to live with grace and mercy as instructed in the inspired written word that the Lord left us.

The Judaizers likely assumed that God's plan and their Jewish nationalistic ambitions were the same. So perhaps, they felt empowered to force their ambitions on the Galatians. But they were in good company! Before Jesus' ascension to the Father, his apostles' question suggested a similar assumption (Acts 1:6-8). In fairness to them all, at that time, God's general plan for the balance of human history was still unfolding. His revelation to John on the island of Patmos was yet to be given.

Fortunately, Jesus had already sown seeds of the kingdom in the disciples (John 20:22). When He selected them to be apostles, they only needed to be in the upper room at Pentecost so the Holy Spirit could germinate those seeds. Much later in human history, as Jesus had revealed through parables, He would return to gather the kingdom harvest. Our heavenly Father knows best!

It's the Lord's Harvest, Not Ours

The church in America has mastered accepting Jesus as Savior and seeking the promises thereof. Unfortunately, we have failed to accept Jesus as Lord and surrender to His teachings. Had we done so, it would preclude any nationalistic ambitions to help the Lord's end-time plans. Here are three reasons why:

1. It is evident in Jesus' parable about the wheat and the weeds, that He does not

welcome our help during the Great Harvest (Matthew 13:24-30).

2. The believer's homeland is heaven, a domain that is universal and not isolated or managed by a nation (2 Corinthians 5:1).

3. The Lord desires that whomever (personal choice) believes in their heart that Jesus is Lord, not compulsory obedience (John 3:16; Romans 10:9-11).

We are so entrenched in self-sufficiency that our capacity to surrender ourselves to Jesus' wisdom, authority, and kingdom principles has gone underdeveloped. Jesus' disciples had gotten it right! Though they were experienced fishermen, after an unproductive all-night fishing expedition, they decided to defer judgment about where to fish to the son of a carpenter (Jesus). The result was a boat load of fish (John 21:1-6). Question: *What made them defer to someone who wasn't even a fisherman?* Answer: *They had room in their perception of who Jesus was to permit it.* Deferring to Him as Lord not only shows that they had accepted His authority, but it also allowed them to experience Jesus' authority over their problem– getting fish. They benefited from surrendering to Jesus' Lordship.

My Side, Your Side, the Lord's Side

Although the Lord is in control, He is also just. Rather than take a particular side amongst Christian factions in conflict, He gives us the dignity to choose to surrender our heart to Him, then choose to take His side. This is depicted clearly in Joshua 5:13-15. I am certain that Joshua was certain that the Lord was on His side. But while on the way to capture the city of Jericho in order to seize the land that the Lord had promised Abraham, he looked up and saw a man standing in front of him with a drawn sword. Confident about the success of his mission, Joshua went up to him and asked, "Are you for us or for our enemies?" Having no doubt that the Lord was on his side, Joshua likely thought the Lord would also give him a victory over this man standing in his way. As it turned out, the man turned out to be an angel who replied to Joshua, "Neither, but as commander of the army of the Lord I have now come." Imagine Joshua's mental distress, having believed that *he* was the one leading the charge to take Jericho. Yet, in front of him was the commander of the Lord's army. Joshua may have reflected on events in the recent past, perhaps wondering

- Did some of my men fail to address the reproach of Egypt that was upon them, as the Lord requested? (See Joshua 5:2-9)

- Did some of my men not celebrate the Passover? (See Joshua 5:10-11)

The Bible does not state why this angel stood in a fighting posture with his sword drawn. He was not there to take Jericho's side. He was not there for Joshua's side. Joshua did not even know the guy! The angel was there to ensure the success of certain divinely ordained events of the Lord's detailed plan for humanity, as He had promised Abraham, Isaac, Jacob, and Moses. It was to Joshua's benefit that he and his men be obedient to what the Lord had required. That would have put them on the Lord's side. Fortunately, Joshua was not so invested in his religious views and tactical prowess that he would not humble himself. So in verse 14, Joshua did the next best thing: he fell down on his face in reverence and then asked, "What message does my Lord have for his servant?"

That is what it looks like to choose the Lord's side, rather than assuming that our obedience compels Him to take our side.

"The sole purpose of life is to gain merit for life in eternity."

\- Augustine of Hippo

Chapter 9: Remain As Salt and Light

Temptation can be subtle, slippery slope interval. Suddenly, you realize that you are free falling into it. We often realize this before we have committed to it. Yet, even by then, it has wrapped its tentacles around our flesh. So, though as a Christian you are weathering America's cultural confusion while standing firmly on the Lord's foundation, think about those Hebrews enslaved in Egypt. They sat securely with houses smeared with lamb's blood. They passed through the parted sea on firm ground. They ate manna from heaven while following the cloud by day and a pillar of fire at night. Then one day, in the wilderness, they found themselves grumbling and rebelling against their deliverer, Moses.

Somewhere, there is a temptation with our name on it. Some of us know what it is, but others may not know what it is. When it slides into your life, remember 1 Corinthians 10:13.

> No temptation has overtaken you except what is common to mankind. And God is faithful; he will not let you be tempted beyond what you can bear. But when you are tempted, he will also provide a way out so that you can endure it.

You and I can build our capacity for enduring such temptation by keeping the following take-aways for remaining salt and light.

Get out of my flesh—The greatest thing we can do to develop greater clarity is not allow the anti-God bias of our culture cause us to feel ashamed about the weapons God has given us to fight with. Our sinful nature has been cultivated to perceive the Lord's weapons as being weak or deficient against the world's problems. Do not make the mistake of resorting back to the weapons of this world. I assure you, anytime we allow the adversary to limit us to their choice of weapons, we will lose. So, for this battle, walking in the Spirit and not in our flesh (5:17) is more than a cliche.

Self-control against getting caught-up - Hate, resentment, and angst will arise. Being in Christ, we are no longer obligated to act on those emotions. Be intentional about not allowing our heart to be reconfigured by these.

Finding strength while weak - The key to our effectiveness when facing conflicts and growing spiritually is to acknowledge our own personal weakness. Though weak and trusting the Lord's strength, we can then discover new capabilities for growth, forgiveness, collaboration, and conflict resolution.

Do not allow contagion to guilt us into overreacting - Before jumping into the cultural fray over controversial matters, consider how much skin we have or intend to put in the viewpoint advocated. Then let that inform how we respond. Beware of peer pressure, especially from other Christians.

Leave probabilities to the statisticians and gamblers - As unlikely as it may seem for you and your adversary to overcome differences, ask yourself, "How much of my doubt is due to my own desire to keep living according to the flesh?" This may reveal areas of your own disobedience in kingdom principles about greetings, kindness, loving, and praying for adversaries (see Matthew 5:44-47).

If it has not worked for me, then do not transport it - Before giving truth to someone, else or correcting them with what the Bible says, ask yourself, "Am I living, or have I lived, what I am about to say?" If not, then either do not transport it to them, or dial down the attitude with which you transport it to them.

Human understanding requires upgrades as well - Although an adversary's point of view may sound very offensive, to effectively refute it, we must identify the kernel of truth (if any) that it hangs on. Because while it may be difficult to accept, there is often a portion of truth in our adversary's beliefs. That is why they can be highly passionate and extreme about proposed remedies. Therefore, each faction could benefit from asking

- Is my version of the truth complete?
- Is belief in this particular truth essential to what it means to be Christian?
- Is it an old truth that has already been debunked?
- Is it true only in certain instances?
- Is it an exaggeration based on fear?
- Can I provide more clarity around that kernel of truth?

The best way to detect a counterfeit is by routinely studying the real thing - Familiarization with Christian theology is essential for equipping believers to remain Christ-centered in a culture with a mishmash of counterfeit views. Before dismantling a falsehood, be sure you have a proper understanding as to why your version is true.

Teach about life in eternity to all ages – What good does it do to teach the good news of Jesus Christ to people who do not believe that they are already in trouble? Teaching the bad news puts meaning and context around the good news. Then teach what can be done now, in order to have the best possible life on earth and hereafter.

Know the villain as soon as possible – Is it them or me? Would it be accurate for the believers who deserted Paul's gospel to claim that the Judaizers were the villains? The Judaizers themselves were ill-informed about the scope of Jesus' redemptive work and the role of the Holy Spirit. All of us are responsible for the implications that come with our choices. That is why it is so important to seek truth, facts, opposing viewpoints, and wise counsel before choosing. Only in doing so can we clearly discern who the villain is in our lives.

That villain, however, may not care about the Bible, Jesus, or the Holy Spirt, but only power and control. So as soon as we can, it is important for us to know the kind of battle we are fighting.

Choosing Jesus' side does not guarantee success in our lifetime – We do not know what happened in the church at Galatia after they received Paul's letter. Nor do we know whether Paul attempted to follow up with the church there. The hope is that success from standing on Jesus' kingdom principles occurred within their lifetime. But the benefits promised us as believers are given by our Lord, who has an eternal perspective. This does not mean He is insensitive about our earthly plight, but that He operates from a different point of view than us. He does see the value in securing the best for us, be it healings, deliverance, vindication, vengeance, abundance, recognition, acceptance, reward, genuine companions, etc., but He decides when that is best (this life or the next). Our earthly lifetime may not accommodate what He desires to secure for us. On the other hand, having no experience with eternal life, you and I tend to want the Lord to secure what we think is best … but within our earthly lifetime.

Can you imagine the confusion in understanding the Bible, due to differences in perspectives about time and eternity? That is why, when we fail to live in time with eternity in mind, we will experience much frustration and confusion. Although it is true that during our lifetime good people often finish last, this is never true for life eternal.

Do not just agree and believe, but also trust – Mentally believing in God is not the same as trusting God. Do not just believe that Jesus teaches us how to live. Do not just agree that, if you pick up your cross and follow Jesus, things would change for the better – and then say, first there are a few things you want to do before you commit to doing so.

Trust is something quite different. Trusting Jesus' teachings is, when you are faced with being obedient to a kingdom principle that you do not want to do, though fearful and trembling, you attempt to obey anyway. Ask yourself, *Has Jesus given us a set of abstract hypothetical propositions for us to acknowledge as best practices? Or, is He expecting us to set out, fearful and trembling, making an attempt to obey Him?* I'm not suggesting that we are able to obey without the help of the Holy Spirit. I am suggesting that we may not be genuine about even attempting to take the initial steps in doing so. Like the question Jesus asked the paralyzed man, "Do you want to get well?" (John 5:6).

Do not become weary of well-doing – It is not so much that all factions are wrong, as much as it is that all factions need Jesus. And the body of Christ (ekklesia) has been uniquely called and equipped to lead them to Jesus. Paul's letter to the Galatians closes with this

Let us not become weary in doing good, for at the proper time we will reap a harvest if we do not give up (Galatians 6:9).

In summary, Jesus is still the Way, Truth and the Life. We, the church in America, need to recenter ourselves in Christ, more than we need new training, tips, tools and techniques (or reimagining). This is not to suggest that change is unnecessary. Because such recentering would be inclusive of changes that result from God's corrective provisions of "teaching, rebuking, correcting and training in righteousness, so that the servant of God may be thoroughly equipped for every good work" (2 Timothy 3:16-17). Then we would be the salt and light of the world that Jesus intended us to be (Matthew 5:13-16).

Bonus: The Bad and Good News

Bad News

- Sin darkens our understanding (Romans 1:20-21).
- Sin prevents us from sensing God's presence (Romans 3:10-11, 23).
- Sin separates us from God (Isaiah 59:2; Ephesians 4:17-19).
- Separation means we are destined for hell forever, after this life (Romans 6:23).

Good News

- Jesus provides sinners with another chance (Romans 5:8).
- Through Jesus, the gift of eternal life is given to those who honestly trust Him in their heart (Romans 10:9-11).
- Faith in Jesus deposits the Holy Spirit in the believer for power and guidance to (Ephesians 1:13-14).

God does not send anyone to hell. From birth, because of Adam's original sin, every human being is destined for hell. Jesus came to save us from this fate, not to condemn us (Matthew 1:21).

About the Author

Jimmie D. Compton, Jr. and his wife Nancy have two children, two grandchildren, and two great-grandchildren. He received a master's degree in Pastoral Counseling from Ashland Theological Seminary and was a licensed therapist for 25 years. In addition to being the founding and Senior Pastor of Hope Bible Fellowship Church for over thirty years, Jimmie also provided counseling services for the Detroit Police Chaplain Corps, Detroit Rescue Mission Ministries, Eastwood Clinic, and New Way Christian Community Church. He has aided dozens of church clergy in biblical, counseling, and ministerial matters while authoring several books. Currently, he is Board Chairman of Citikidz Christian Sports Camp in Rector, PA. He loves running, walking, working out, and mentoring young men in his neighborhood.

Jimmie has been honored for completing an in-depth, six-year research project, *Early African Church History: From Jesus' Resurrection to the Rise of Islam*. This research has been developed into a two-year, online, self-paced curriculum at Hope Institute, the teaching and ministerial arm of Hope Bible Fellowship Church.

Books by the Author

In addition to paperback, *Ball of Confusion in Galatia* is also available on Kindle and Audible. For bulk purchases, please email us at hbf.church@gmail.com with the title in the subject line. You can find descriptions of Jimmie's other works and purchase them at amazon.com/author/jimmiecompton.

Endnotes

[1] As evidenced by Acts 6:6-14, 15:5, 21-28, 23:12-35, after Jesus' ascension it was not uncommon for non-Messianic-Jews teachers of the law to attempt to eradicate the church from the outside. There were also Jewish teachers of the law who had become members of the church (infiltrators – Acts 15:1, Galatians 2:4). Though in the previous scripture Apostle Paul referred to the latter as "false believers", it is unclear whether he does so because of their benign lack of spiritual insight, or because they had intentionally faked their belief in order to undermine the church. Either way, their message was extremely damaging to the truth of the gospel. By referring to them as Messianic-Jews I am giving them the benefit of the doubt.

[2] Phillip Schaff, *History of the Christian Church*, Vol. 7, (Grand Rapids: W.M. Eerdmans Publishing Co., 1910), 650-653.

[3] "Press Briefing by Press Secretary Dana Perino," The White House: President George W. Bush, January 7, 2009, https://georgewbush-whitehouse.archives.gov/news/releases/2009/01/20090107.html.

[4] Scot McKnight, *The NIV Application Commentary: Galatians* (Grand Rapids, MI: Zondervan Publishing House, 1995), 23.

[5] Ibid., 24.

[6] Ibid., 31.

[7] Ibid., 30.

[8] Ibid., 25.

[9] Ibid.

[10] Ibid.

[11] Ibid., 26.

[12] Francis Waton, Paul, Judaism, and the Gentiles: Beyond the New Perspective (Grand Rapids, MI: Wm B. Eerdmans Publishing Co, 2007), 46.

www.ingramcontent.com/pod-product-compliance
Lightning Source LLC
Chambersburg PA
CBHW071908020426
42331CB00010B/2712